KB090373

English
for Flight
Attendants

Kim Soo Jung

BAEKSAN Publishing Co

Preface

『English for Flight Attendants』는 실제 공항 및 기내에서 객실승무원이 사용하는 살아 있는 영어를 습득함을 목표로 한다. 이미 영어는 우리 사회에서 일상생활에서도 흔히 사용할 정도가 되었으며, 하물며 외국인 승객과의 접점에 있는 객실승무원의 영어 실력의 중요성에 대해서는 말할 필요가 없을 것이다. 이 책은 가능한 한 실용성에 초점을 두고 실제로 말하는 방법을 연습하는 과정에 중점을 두었다. 그렇기 때문에 이 책에서는 용법 하나하나를 개별적으로 설명하고 모범 답안을 제시하기보다, 학생들이 앞으로 객실승무원으로 근무하게 될 때에 마주칠 상황에 대하여 직접 생각해보고 말하기 연습을 할 수 있는 워크북의 형태로 만들었다.

항공사들의 동맹(alliance), 공동운항(Code-sharing), 나아가 글로벌화 등으로 국내 항공사의 국내선 구간에도 점차 외국인 승객수가 증가하고 있고, 앞으로도 이 추세는 더 늘어날 전망이다. 아무쪼록 이 교재를 통해 학생들이 틀에 박힌 천편일률적인 딱딱한 영어 문장이 아닌, 본인의 생각을 편안하고 자유롭게 영어로 구사할 수 있게 되기를 바란다. 또한 국·내외 항공사 취업을 준비하는 데도 유용하게 활용하여 각자 원하는 목표를 이루어나가는 디딤돌이 되기를 기원한다.

저 자

Contents

D International Departures

Introduction

1

Starter

1. Who are flight attendants?

2. Why do people want to become cabin crew?

3. What are the good points and bad points about the job? Complete the chart below.

Good Points	Bad Points

█istening

Listen to the flight attendant talk about her job and choose T(true) or F(false).

1. The flight attendant's main responsibility is passenger safety.　　T / F

2. The job is easy to do.　　T / F

█id You Know?

Different countries, airlines, and sizes of aircraft can all have different names for cabin crew jobs.

Chief Purser(CP) / Senior Purser(SP) / Cabin Service Manager(CSM) / Inflight Service Manager(ISM)

Inflight Supervisor(IFS) / Inflight Service Director(ISD) are mainly found on larger aircraft types and are in charge of the running of the cabin.

Chief Pursers are flight attendants that have been promoted through the ranks-Flight attendant → Senior flight attendant → Purser → Chief Purser.

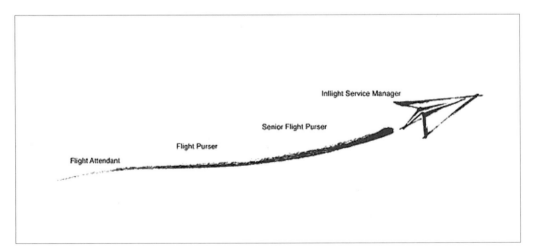

www.cathaypacific.com

Build Up

Read the following and match with the job below.

1. _____ report when the cabin is secure for takeoff and landing and any broken or missing emergency equipment items to the pilots after the preflight check. They generally operate the doors during routine, account for all money and required paperwork and report for each flight. They are in charge of the whole cabin.

2. _____ assist the Chief Purser and have similar roles and responsibilities.

3. _____ are the ones who gain experience as a flight attendant for two to five years. They work in the Business and First class cabin and they are usually in charge of the each galley.

4. _____ must pass the safety training upon employment. They usually work in the Economy class cabin and report to the senior crew.

*Flight Attendant	*Senior Flight Attendant	*Purser	*Chief Purser

Did You Know?

Economy Class

Emirates Airline A380–800

File : American Airlines Boeing 777–200 Seat Plan.gif. From Wikipedia, the free encyclopedia

It is also known as coach class. These are standard seats and the food service is standard, too. There isn't much leg room, but every seat has a seat-back video screen for movies and games nowadays.

Business Class

Gulf Air

It was originally intended as an intermediate level of service between economy class and first class. Business class is distinguished from other travel classes by the quality of seating, food, drinks, ground service and other amenities.

First Class

Cathay Pacific B747-400

First class is a luxury travel class on some airliners that exceeds business class and economy class. The passengers in this class expect a very high standard of comfort and service. It begins with special priority check-in and a dedicated lounge with complimentary food and drink. The seats can be converted to fully flat private beds.

Build Up

What do you know about classes of airline travel? Mark which classes offer which amenities

Amenities	Economy Class	Business Class	First Class
1. A lot of leg room			
2. High quality food and drink service			
3. Standard food and drink service			
4. Seat-back video			
5. Priority check-in			
6. A dedicated lounge			
7. A standard seat			
8. A fully flat bed			

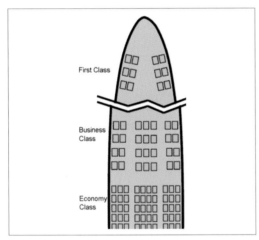

Boeing 747 Seat Configuration

File : American Airlines Boeing 777−200 Seat Plan.gif. From Wikipedia. the free encyclopedia

Vocabulary

Fill blanks with a right word from the box below.

*captain	*check in	*passport	*maintenance	*security check
*control tower	*baggage claim	*immigration	*passenger	*ramp

1. The _____ has cleared the aircraft for landing.

2. The delayed aircraft is finally approaching the _____.

3. You need to fill out this _____ form before we arrive Korea.

4. People can collect their luggage at the _____ area.

5. A person needs a _____ to enter foreign countries.

6. The pilot had to decide to divert the aircraft due to _____ problem.

7. Everyone has to go through the _____ point before boarding.

8. Please _____ 2 hours prior to departure.

9. The _____ explained that the plane could not land until the storm had passed over the runway via PA.

10. The _____ press the call button to ask some water to a flight attendant.

Reading

What is Service?

Service is all those activities and beliefs that develop relationships between an organization and its passengers. Business often fails because of the failure to establish[1] and maintain good relations with customers.

Developing relationships requires a proactive[2] effort. It is important to work hard at cultivating[3] good service relationships with your passengers.

It is not difficult to develop the skills needed to enhance customer relationships. To do so, ask yourself these questions and respond:

✓ What do passengers want?
✓ Why do they want the service?
✓ When do they want it?
✓ How do I differentiate my product (service) from others?
✓ What must I do to meet and then exceed customers' expectations?

You need to develop good service relationships with your passengers by listening to and translating their needs into a service that fulfills their needs. Passengers have the need to be in a safe and caring environment during their flight and upon arrival. Their needs should be met immediately. If it is difficult

---

[1] establish : 수립하다
[2] proactive : 앞을 내다보고 행동하는
[3] cultivate : 기르다, 계발하다

to meet the need, the harder you try, the more passenger can see the attempt made to please him, the more grateful he will be for your effort.

Think of the passenger encounter[4] as an "experience". Focus on how to make his/her experience a memorable and pleasurable one. No matter how you may feel or what has happened, the passenger comes first. Remember what really counts is the ATTITUDE with which the passenger is treated and this is demonstrated through being consistently caring and helpful to provide quality service.

[4] encounter : 마주치다

D International Departures

↓

Airline Office
& Airport Service

2

Starter

Look at the pictures and choose the right word from the box.

1.

_____

2.

_____

3.

_____

4.

_____

5.

_____

6.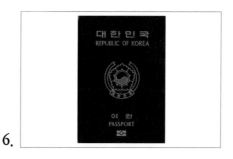

_____

*baggage claim tag	*boarding pass	*cart
*passport	*baggage carousel	*trolley bag

Think About

Cabin crew work closely with other aviation professionals such as

Captain

First officer

Maintenance (apron/ramp service)

Cabin service

Catering

Passenger service staff

Why would a cabin crew member need to communicate with them?

Did You Know

An **electronic ticket** (commonly abbreviated[5] as **e-ticket**) is a digital ticket. In the case of an airline ticket, the e-ticket rapidly replaced the older multi-layered paper tickets and became mandatory[6] for IATA[7] members as from June 1, 2008. Once a reservation is made, an e-ticket exists only as a digital record in the airline computers. It is also possible to print multiple copies of an e-ticket itinerary[8] receipt; hence the "loss" of an airline ticket becomes impossible. To check in with an e-ticket, the passenger usually goes to the check-in counter and presents a government-issued ID, credit card or the e-ticket itinerary receipt which contains a confirmation or reservation code.

---

5 abbreviated : 단축된, 생략된
6 mandatory : 의무의, 필수의
7 IATA : International Air Transport Association 국제 민간 항공 수송 협회
8 itinerary : 여행 스케줄, 여정

Vocabulary

Fill blanks with a right word from the box below.

*departure	*round-trip	*aisle	*delay	*seating arrangement
*check-in	*in advance	*destination	*boarding	*reservation

1. Air fares are cheaper when you buy _____.

2. Passengers must be at the airport at least 2 hours before _____.

3. It costs 300 dollars single and 500 dollars _____.

4. I like to sit on _____ seat because I don't enjoy looking out the window.

5. There will be a _____ in the departure of our plane.

6. _____ are made at check-in.

7. All passengers please report to Gate 12 for _____.

8. After _____, passengers proceed to the aircraft with their boarding pass.

9. Rome is one of the most popular tourist _____s in the world.

10. Can I change my _____ to a different date?

Conversation 1   *- Jessica Speaking*

Listen and practice.

A : Agent	P : Passenger

A : Good morning, Asea Airlines, Jessica speaking. How may I help you?

P : Hello. I'd like to make a flight reservation to New York.

A : When would you like to travel, sir?

P : Next Monday.

A : We have a few seats available on AS 012.

It departs at 9:00 am and arrives in New York at 12:30 pm the same day.

Is that all right?

P : Good.

A : Which class would you like to take?

P : I'd like to reserve an economy seat.

A : May I have your name and phone number, please?

P : David Hines, 010-9123-1234.

A : All right, Mr. Hines.

Your flight is AS 012 at 9:00 am on May 2nd Monday on economy.

Is there anything I can help you more?

P : No, that's all. Thank you.

A : Thank you for calling, Asea Airlines.

ⒷBuild-up 1

다음의 우리말을 참고하여 영어로 말해보세요.

A : Good morning, (your name) speaking.
　　어떻게 도와드릴까요?

_____

B : Good morning.
　　LA로 가는 비행기 표를 예약하고 싶습니다.

_____

A : 언제 여행하실 예정이세요?

_____

B : Next Monday.

A : AS 014편에 몇 자리 가능합니다.

_____

　　It departs at 7:00 pm and 같은 날 오전 11시 30분에 LA에 도착합니다.

_____

　　Is that all right?

B : Good.

A : 어느 클래스로 여행하기 원하십니까?

_____

B : I'd like to reserve a business, please.

A : 성함과 전화번호를 말씀해 주시겠습니까?

_____

B : _____, 010-9123-1234.

A : All right, (the name of the passenger).
　　7월 10일 월요일 오후 7시에 LA로 출발하는 AS 014편입니다.

_____

　　Is there anything I can help you more?

B : No, that's all. Thank you.

Conversation 2   *- Do you have any baggage to check in?*

Listen and practice

A : Good morning, sir. May I see your passport and ticket, please?

P : Here you are.

A : Thank you. Are you going to New York, Mr. Hines?

P : That's right. Is the flight going to depart on time?

A : Yes, sir. It is on time.

    Would you like an aisle or a window seat?

P : I'd like to get a seat by the window.

A : No, problem, sir. Do you have any baggage to check-in?

P : Yes, I have one bag to check-in.

A : All right. Here is your baggage tag and your boarding pass.

    Your boarding starts at 8:30 from Gate 12. Your seat number is 38A.

P : Thank you.

A : My pleasure, Mr. Hines. Have a good trip.

Build-up 2

다음의 우리말을 참고하여 영어로 말해보세요.

A : Good morning, sir. 여권과 티켓을 보여주시겠습니까?

_____

B : Here you are.

A : Thank you. 뉴욕으로 가는 _____ 씨 맞으십니까?

_____

B : That's right. Is the flight going to depart on time?

A : Yes, sir. It is on time.

통로와 창측 어느 쪽이 더 좋으십니까?

_____

B : I'd like to get a seat by the window.

A : No, problem, sir. 부치실 짐이 있으십니까?

_____

B : Yes, I have one bag to check-in.

A : All right. Here is your baggage tag and your boarding pass.

20번 게이트에서 9시부터 탑승이 시작됩니다.

_____

Your seat number is 42A.

B : Thank you.

A : 천만에요, _____씨. 즐거운 여행되세요.

_____

Think About

1. What would you say if a passenger wants a seat by the emergency exit?

2. What would you say if the flight is delayed?

Useful Expressions

We have two flights on that day.

How many are there in your party?

Do you have any seat preferences?

Sorry, we are slightly behind schedule.

We have full load today.

Do you have anything fragile?

Reading

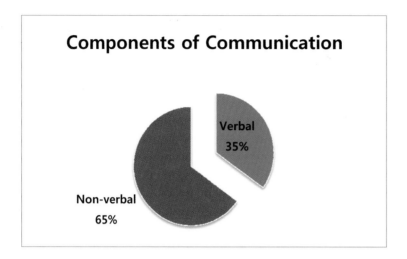

Body Language

Body language is a form of mental and physical ability of human non-verbal communication, which consists of body posture[9], gestures, facial expressions, and eye movements. Humans send and interpret such signals almost entirely subconsciously[10].

Important aspects of body language

1. Tone of Voice

Variations of tone affect the meaning of speech and reveal the emotional state of the speaker – whether he is genuine, sarcastic[11], irritated or disrespectful. The pitch of voice, loud or gentle, affects the meaning of speech as well. The speech tone should be pleasant and varied.

---

[9] posture : 자세
[10] subconsciously : 잠재의식적으로
[11] sarcastic : 빈정대는, 비꼬는, 냉소적인

2. Facial expression

Facial expression gives a continuous commentary[12] on the true feelings of the speaker and the listener. A smile is most effective when greeting passengers, serving them and taking their orders as it conveys warmth and pleasure. A smile can partly replace words.

3. Eye contact

Looking and eye contact play several important roles. People look to obtain information and feedback from others. The act of looking also indicates[13] the amount and kind of interest the looker has at the other. Maintaining eye contact is also a form of attentiveness[14] and courteous[15] behavior.

4. Gestures

Hand gestures are closely linked to speech and can affect the meaning of what you say. When a passenger is angry and you respond by folding your arms, you may make him angrier.

5. Posture

Posture is one of the main body signals showing attitude towards another person. Having a slight-forward leaning body posture while you are talking to a passenger gives a friendly impression.

6. Appearance

Physical grooming, cleanliness and clothes reveal your attitude and your pride in work. You should maintain a neat personal appearance.

---

12 commentary : 설명
13 indicate : 나타내다, 가리키다
14 attentiveness : 주의 깊게 주의를 기울임
15 courteous : 예의바른, 정중한

D International Departures

↓

Pre-flight

3

Starter

What makes good flight attendants?

____ Good eye contact

____ Excellent grammar

____ Arrogant posture

____ A seductive look

____ A pleasant smile

____ A clear, confident voice

____ Expensive clothes and nice jewelry

____ A very serious attitude about everything

____ A very informal way of speaking

____ Comfortable but polite communication

____ A caring mind

____ A positive body language

Small Talk

1. What qualities do you have now that will help you be a good cabin crew?

2. What qualities do you need to develop?

Did You Know?

A passport is an official documents issued by a government to identify the bearer as a citizen or a permanent resident of the issuing country. A visa is a permit by an official of a government to indicate that the bearer has been granted authority to enter or re-enter the country concerned. Not all countries require a visa.

Vocabulary

Complete the chart with service items and safety equipment. Refer to the pictures on the next page.

Service Items	Safety Equipment

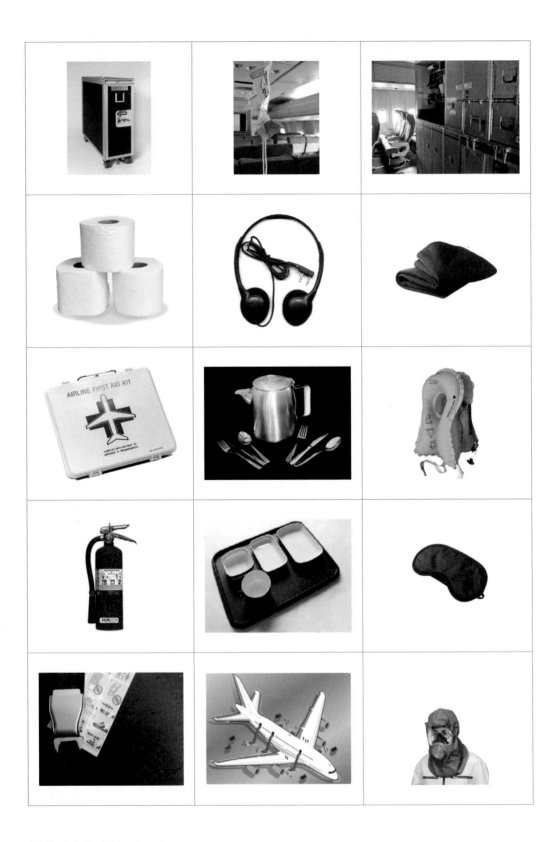

Build Up

Answer these questions.

✓ Why do passengers expect?

✓ What do passengers want?

✓ When do they want it?

✓ How do I differentiate my product (service) from the others?

✓ What must I do to meet and then exceed customers' expectations?

Can you give examples of following service?

1. Warm service

   _____

2. Caring service

   _____

3. Efficient service

   _____

4. Enterprising service

   _____

5. Dedicated service

   _____

Cabin Service Procedures

What does cabin crew prepare for each step?

Service Procedures	Things to Do
1. Before Boarding	
2. Boarding	
3. Before Take-off	
4. Cruising	
5. Landing	

Listening

Listen to cabin crew briefing and answer the questions.

1. Who is the purser today? _____

2. What is the flight number? _____

3. Where is the flight going to? _____

4. What is the departure time? _____

5. What do crew need to check before flight? _____

Think About

Why is pre-flight briefing important for crew?

Reading

항공기 비상 착륙, 또는 착수 시에는 어느 때보다 승무원의 역할이 중요합니다. 비상사태 발생시 사용하는 승무원의 명령문을 영어로 연습해 봅시다.

Specific Commands

Each emergency situation is essentially a unique incident. No procedures can include all possible types of accidents or emergency situations. Neither is it possible to dictate the exact steps to follow in such situations.

In any emergency situation, Cabin Crew should, in most circumstances, start an emergency procedure only after an order from the Captain. However, in cases which are clearly catastrophic[16], individual crewmembers should be prepared to act immediately on their own initiative.

Commands given here are used to instruct passenger to adopt the brace position and enhance serviceability during an aircraft impact. They should be used in response to the situation at hand.

When signaled by the Tech Crew this command should be given by Cabin Crew before impact.

> BEND OVER! HEADS DOWN!
> STAY DOWN! BEND OVER!
> STAY DOWN!

Conduct the evacuation in an assertive[17] manner. Direct passengers through aircraft exits when they are opened. Give loud, short, clear commands so as

---

16 catastrophic : 비극적인, 비참한
17 assertive : 단호한

to establish authority. Commands must be simple, be easily followed and appropriate to the situation. Avoid negative commands such as "DO NOT WAIT" or "DON'T GO THERE"

During evacuation, the crew must monitor the conditions of the exits and, if required, stop evacuation through those exits which become unsafe due to spreading of fire or damage of the slides.

```
                    OPEN SEAT BELT!
                        MOVE!
                  COME THIS WAY! JUMP!
```

If an exit is not useable the crew must direct passengers to the nearest usable exits.

```
                       NO EXIT!
                GO BACK! GO FORWARD!
                      GO ACROSS!
```

In a ditching emergency, it is paramount that all passengers put on their life vests.

```
                    OPEN SEAT BELT!
                 LIFE VEST UNDER SEAT!
                    PUT ON LIFE VEST!
                     TAKEOFF SHOES!
```

Other useful commands,

```
                   GET OUT OF SEATS!
                   GO! JUMP! MOVE!
                    DOOR JAMMED!
                       NO SLIDE!
```

International Departures

D

Boarding &

Cabin Preparation for Take-off

4

Starter

How would you greet passengers on board?

Hello.
Welcome aboard.

Listening

Listen to the flight attendant greeting a passenger and answer the questions.

1. Is the plane full? _____

2. Why is the passenger upset? _____

3. What will the flight attendant do? _____

Did You Know

www.airfrance.com

It is important for cabin crew to notice their first impression of boarding passengers. They need to be aware of passengers who may have problems, or cause problems, during a flight. What can you as a flight attendant do to prepare for or avoid in-flight problems?

Vocabulary

Fill blanks with a right word from the box below.

*mind	*fasten	*overhead bin	*take off	*upright
*device	*belongings	*clear	*bassinet	*separated

1. Can I use electronic _____ s on the plane?

2. Please stow your carry-on items in the _____.

3. Do you _____ if I open the window shade?

4. Could you _____ your seat belt?

5. Don't forget to take all of your personal _____ with you.

6. In preparation for _____, I'd like to ask you to turn off your hand phone.

7. Would you please return your seat to the _____ position?

8. Do you need a _____ for your baby?

9. Aisles must keep _____ all the time.

10. My wife and I are _____. Can we sit together?

Conversation 1   *- Welcome aboard.*

Listen and practice

F/A : Flight attendant	P : Passenger

F/A : Good morning. Welcome aboard.

　　　May I see your boarding pass, please?

P1　 : Yes, here you are.

F/A : Thank you. Please go across and turn right.

P1　 : Thank you.

P2　 : Excuse me, where is my seat?

F/A : Let me see your boarding pass, please.

　　　Thank you. Your seat is 32B.

　　　This way, please. Here we are.

　　　Would you please keep your bag in the overhead bin?

Emirates A380 Economy Class Cabin

■Build-up 1

다음의 우리말을 참고하여 영어로 말해보세요.

A : 안녕하십니까. 어서 오십시오.

_____

탑승권을 보여주시겠습니까?

_____

B : Yes, here you are.
A : Thank you. 이쪽으로 가십시오.

_____

B : Thank you.
C : Excuse me, where is my seat?
A : 제가 탑승권을 좀 봐도 되겠습니까?

_____

Thank you. Your seat is 45H.
저를 따라 오십시오. 손님의 자리는 여기입니다.

_____

짐을 머리 위 선반에 보관해 주시겠습니까?

_____

Think About

1. What would you do if there is a couple who is asking for seats together when the flight is full?

```
```

2. How would you help a blind passenger for boarding?

```
```

Useful Expressions

Come this way.

Go straight down.

Take the aisle to the left.

Let me show you to your seat.

Your seat is in the back of the cabin.

Another cabin attendant will help you there.

Your seat is two rows behind.

Would you mind changing your seat for the couple who are separated?

It would be appreciated if you would not mind changing your seat for him.

Conversation 2   *- We are going to take off soon.*

Listen and practice

F/A : Excuse me, sir. Is this bag yours?

P   : Yes, it is.

F/A : Sir, we have to keep the aisle clear.

Would you want me to stow your bag in the overhead bin?

P   : Oh, I'm sorry. Thank you.

F/A : That's alright.

Please fasten your seatbelt, and return your seat to the upright position.

We are going to take off soon.

■Build-up 2

아래의 구문을 사용하여 다음의 우리말을 영어로 바꾸어 보세요.

정중하게 말하기	정중하지만 단호하게 말하기	강하게 말하거나 지시하기
Is it all right if …?	Could you …?	Put it in the …
Would you mind helping me with …?	Can you please …?	Don't …
Would it possible to …?	I'd like you to …	Will you …?
Could you possibly …?	I want you to …, please.	Sit down!

제가 손님의 코트를 객실 뒤쪽 (at the back of the cabin)에 보관해 드려도 되겠습니까?

_____

손님의 짐을 좌석 밑 (under the seat in front of you)에 넣어주시겠습니까?

_____

좌석벨트를 매주십시오.

_____

짐을 넣을 수 있게 저를 좀 도와주시겠습니까?

_____

자리에 앉으십시오!

_____

■Think About

1. What would you say to a passenger who uses the phone?

```



```

2. What should you do to passengers who are seated in the emergency exit row?

```



```

Reading

When Passengers Board

There are several general duties that have to be performed before the passengers start to board the aircraft. You must make sure that all doors and aisles are free from obstruction[18]. You should check that the stairs or aerobridge[19] are properly positioned and safe for passengers to use when entering the aircraft. You must check that the food and drinks supplies and equipment have been stored properly.

As the passengers enter the aircraft, the cabin crew should greet them, help

---

[18] obstruction : 방해물, 장애물
[19] aerobridge : 공항 대합실과 항공기를 연결하는 통로

them find their seats and put their hand luggage in the overhead lockers.

Once the passengers have boarded the aircraft, the cabin crew must perform their duties efficiently but politely. You may occasionally have to make announcements, although this is normally the job of a designated[20] announcer. You must also make sure that the seats next to emergency exits are taken by able-bodied[21] adults, in case of an emergency. A passenger head count must be carried out for security reasons.

The cabin crew is also responsible for the closing and locking of doors and must communicate with the captain through the in-flight purser. The take-off positions for cabin crew may be jump seats. These seats are located near exits and folded away when not in use.

All the passengers and crew should remain seated until there is a warning from the flight crew. If any passenger does not comply with[22] this safety regulation, you should direct the passenger to remain seated with a verbal warning.

---

[20] designate : 명시하다, 지명하다
[21] able-bodied : An **able-bodied** person is physically strong and healthy, rather than weak or disabled.
[22] comly with : 규칙에 따르다

D International Departures

↓

Beverage
Service

5

Starter

There are many different kinds of drink on board. Look at the list of drinks and put them in the correct category.

*Perrier *soda *orange juice *Cognac *Merlot *vodka *diet Coke *ginger ale
*Espresso *green tea *Bacardi *Absolute *port *Bloody Mary *chamomile
*mineral water *Earl Grey *Martini *Dom Perignon *cappuccino *gin *toni
*water *Budweiser *bourbon *gin *whisky *still water *ginseng tea *chardonnay

Wines and beers	Spirits
Soft drinks	Hot drinks

Listening

Listen to the flight attendant serving drinks to three passengers. Put the drinks in the order you hear them asked for.

a. _____ A cup of coffee

b. _____ A glass of water

c. _____ A glass of orange juice

d. _____ A gin and tonic

e. _____ A glass of apple juice

Small Talk

1. What drinks do you like and dislike?

2. What would you drink on board as a passenger?

Did You Know

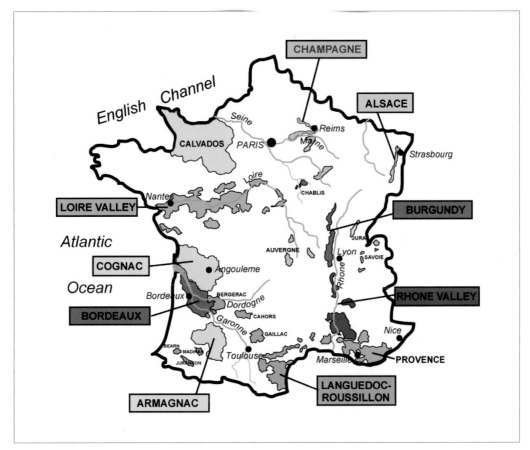

French wine region map

Burgundy and Bordeaux are famous regions in France which produce very good quality wines. The region of Champagne produces champagne of high quality. All champagne are sparkling wine but not all sparkling wines are champagne.

Vocabulary

It's well known that fancy western meals are multi-course. What is each of the courses, and in what order are they supposed to be served? Choose the words from the box.

*aperitif	*wine	*soup	*appetizer	*bread
*garnish	*cheese	*dressings	*dessert	*appetite

1. _____ is present throughout the meal as a matter of course. The French view it as a symbol of hospitality, and would never serve a meal without it.

2. _____ is the classic beverage of choice for meals, and is available readily.

3. _____ (Hors D'oeuvres) : This is a starter.

These are meant to stimulate the **4.** _____ .

They're traditionally served first, sometimes with a small cocktail called an **5.**

_____ .

6. _____ : This is a liquid cooked food containing small pieces of meat, fish or vegetable.

Traditionally, simple greens tossed with **7.** _____ are served as a means of cleansing the palate and aiding digestion.

The Main Course (Entrée) : The main dish of a meal. An elaborate meat, seafood or poultry dish accompanied by a vegetable **8.** _____ will be served.

The **9.** _____ Plate : After dinner they appreciate a selection of it served on a wooden board with assorted cut fruit. This signals the end of a casual, family-style meal.

The **10.** _____ Course : Sweet foods served after main part of the meal. Special occasions call for a treat. What a fantastic way to end a formal meal!

Conversation 1   *- Would you like something to drink?*

Listen and practice

F/A : Excuse me, sir. Would you like something to drink?

P   : Ah, yes. What do you have?

F/A : We have soft drinks, fruit juice, wines, beers and cocktails.

P   : What kind of soft drinks do you have?

F/A : There are coke, 7-up, ginger ale[23], and soda water, sir.

P   : I'll have a can of coke, please.

F/A : Certainly, sir. Would you care for some ice with your coke?

P   : Yes, please.

F/A : Here you are. Enjoy your drink, sir.

P   : Thank you.

---

[23] ginger ale : 생강 맛을 들인 청량 탄산음료

Build-up 1

다음의 우리말을 참고하여 영어로 말해 보세요.

A : Excuse me, sir. 어떤 음료를 하시겠습니까?

_____

B : Ah, yes. What do you have?

A : 탄산음료, 과일주스, 와인, 맥주 등이 준비되어 있습니다.

_____

B : What kind of cocktails do you have?

A : Screw Driver, Bloody Mary, Gin & Tonic, Manhattan, Martini 등이 있습니다.

_____

B : I'll have a _____, please.

A : 알겠습니다. 함께 드실 땅콩도 좀 드릴까요?

_____

B : Yes, please.

A : 여기 있습니다. 맛있게 드십시오.

_____

B : Thank you.

Conversation 2 *- Could you tell me how it is made?*

Listen and practice

F/A : Excuse me, sir. Would you care for something to drink?

P   : Yes, I'd like to have a Black Russian.

F/A : Oh, I am afraid I don't know that drink, sir.

Could you tell me how it is made?

P   : Sure. It is a shot of Kahlua and two shots of vodka with ice.

F/A : Alright, sir.

Here is your drink. Tell me if it is too strong or too weak.

P   : That's good. Thank you.

F/A : It's my pleasure. Enjoy your drink.

◨Build-up 2

다음의 우리말을 참고하여 영어로 말해 보세요.

A : Excuse me, sir. 식전에 음료 한잔 하시겠습니까?

_____

B : Yes, I'd like to have a glass of Black Russian.

A : 죄송합니다만, 그게 무슨 음료인지 잘 모르겠습니다.

_____

만드는 방법을 말씀해 주시겠습니까?

_____

B : Sure. It is a shot of Kahlua and two shots of vodka with ice.

A : Alright, sir.

음료 여기 있습니다.

_____

맛이 너무 강하거나 약하면 말씀해 주십시오.

_____

B : That's good. Thank you.

A : It's my pleasure. Enjoy your drink.

Think About

1. What would you do if a passenger asks you a hot drink when bar service?

2. What would you say if a passenger says he is very hungry at the time of drink service?

Useful expressions

Practice these sentences with smile.

What would you like to drink?

Would you like anything to drink?

Can I offer you a drink?

What can I get you?

I will get it for you, right away.

Reading

The serving of Wine

If you observe the serving of wine in reputed[24] restaurants, you will see that it is done in an elegant and ceremonious[25] manner. A typical scene would have the wine server first presenting the wine to the diner. This is for him or her to sight the label and approve of his or her choice. The wine is then uncorked in the presence of the diner and a little is poured into the wine glass for the host diner to taste. After viewing the wine, twirling[26] the glass, sniffing[27] the aroma and tasting, the host finally nods his approval to the wine server to serve the wine. The significance wine plays in complementing[28] the meal and the ambience[29] cannot be underestimated[30].

With such rituals attached to the serving of wine, it is important that we learn to serve wine correctly. The guides to the correct method of serving of wine must therefore be strictly adhered to.

---

24 reputed : 평판이 좋은, 유명한
25 ceremonious : 예의 바른, 의식(儀式)적인
26 twirl : 빙빙 돌리다
27 sniff : 냄새를 맡다
28 complementing : 보완하는
29 ambience : 분위기, 환경
30 underestimate : 과소평가하다

D International Departures

Meal Service

6

Starter

Label the objects on the meal tray.

❶ _____

❷ _____

❸ _____

❹ _____

❺ _____

❻ _____

❼ _____

❽ _____

Listening

Listen to the flight attendant serving the meal to passengers and answer the questions.

1. What does a passenger want for her meal? _____

2. Does a passenger like spicy food? _____

3. What does a passenger drink with her meal? _____

Small Talk

Think of a time when you were a customer in a restaurant or hotel.

Did you get good service or bad service? What happened?

Why was the service good or bad?

Vocabulary

Fill blanks with a right word from the box below.

*refreshments / snacks	*entrée / main course	*starter / appetizer
*breakfast *lunch	*dinner *dessert	

Many meals are served on the aircraft. The type of meal depends on:

✓ Whether the passenger is in first, business or economy class

✓ The length of the sector

✓ The time of day

1. _____ may consist of a croissant with jam, with fruit juice and tea or coffee. It may be a larger cooked meal.

2. _____ and 3. _____ more substantial meals. For 4. _____ there may be soup or hors d'oeuvres. The 5. _____ is either a meat dish (such as beef) or fish (for example salmon), followed by 6. _____ .

7. _____ range from open sandwiches or fresh fruit to packets of biscuits or nuts.

Food served to economy class passengers may be pre-set, i.e. prepared fully or partially by a kitchen at the airport. Pre-packed hot meals are often supplied by the kitchen. These have to be re-heated before being added to the serving tray.

Conversation 1   - *Which one would you like?*

Listen and practice.

F/A : Good evening, ma'am.

We are serving Korean style beef with rice and braised[31] chicken with potato for your dinner.

Which one would you like?

P   : How is the beef cooked? Is it very spicy?

F/A : No, it's marinated[32] with soy sauce. Would you like to try it?

P   : Yes, please.

F/A : Okay. Would you please open your tray table?

Would you care for a glass of wine with your beef?

P   : Yes. Red, please.

F/A : All right. Here you go.

Enjoy your meal, ma'am.

---

31 braise : When you **braise** meat or a vegetable, you fry it quickly and then cook it slowly in a covered dish with a small amount of liquid.

32 marinate : If you **marinate** meat or fish, or if it **marinates**, you keep it in a mixture of oil, vinegar, spices, and herbs, before cooking it, so that it can develop a special flavor.

Build-up 1

다음의 우리말을 참고하여 영어로 말해 보세요.

A : Good evening, ma'am.
한국식 비빔밥과 크림소스 해물 파스타가 준비되어 있습니다.

_____

어느 것으로 하시겠습니까?

_____

B : How is Korean Bibimbap cooked? Is it very spicy?
A : No, 비빔밥은 여러 가지 야채를 밥에 넣고 고추장에 비벼 드시면 됩니다.

_____

매운 게 싫으시다면, 고추장을 넣지 않으시면 됩니다.

_____

한 번 드셔 보시겠어요?

_____

B : Yes, please.
A : Okay. 제가 테이블을 펴 드릴까요?

_____

함께 드실 와인 좀 드릴까요?

_____

B : Yes. Red, please.
A : All right. Here you go.
맛있게 드세요.

_____

Think About

1. What would you do if the choice of a meal runs out?

2. What would you do if a passenger asks you an additional main course?

Useful Expressions

Practice these sentences with smile.

What would you like for your dinner?

May I offer you a meal?

It is grilled beef served with creamy mushroom sauce.

Bibimbap is steamed rice with cooked vegetables and red pepper paste.

Let me open your table.

Here we are.

There you are.

Try This!

기내에는 다양한 종류의 특별식이 탑재됩니다. 아래의 기내 특별식 명칭을 한국어로 바꾸어 보세요.

1. Bland Meal (BLML) _____

2. Diabetic Meal (DBML) _____

3. Gluten-free Meal (GFML) _____

4. Low Fat/Cholesterol (LFML/LCML) _____

5. Low Sodium Meal (LSML) _____

6. Peanut Free Meal (PFML) _____

7. Hindu Meal (HNML) _____

8. Kosher (KSML) _____

9. Muslim Meal (MOML) _____

10. Vegetarian Meal (VGML) _____

Did You Know

The flight crew-the captain, the first officer and the second officer usually are given different foods to reduce the risk that all might become ill at the same time. On some airlines, the flight crew is not permitted to eat shellfish, due to the risk of food poisoning.

Conversation 2 — *- I'll check on that immediately.*

Listen and practice

F/A : Would you like beef or chicken, sir?

P   : Do you have any vegetarian meals on board?
   I requested a vegetarian meal when I made a reservation.

F/A : Oh, I'm sorry, sir. I will check on that immediately.
   May I have your name, please?

P   : David Hines.

F/A : All right, Mr. Hines. I will be back in a short while.
   (···)
   Thank you for waiting, Mr. Hines. We have your vegetarian meal.
   I'm sorry for the inconvenience.
   Do you need anything else?

P   : Can I have a cup of coffee?

F/A : We will serve coffee and tea right
   after the meal service.
   Would that be alright?

P   : Sure. I will wait for that.

F/A : Thank you, sir. Enjoy your meal.

Think About

1. What would you say if a passenger sees a foreign object[33] in his meal?

2. A passenger brought to your attention that he has made a special meal request. You've checked and found that no such request was reflected in your SPML list. What would you say or do?

3. A passenger indicated he is a vegetarian and cannot eat those featured in the menu. What would you do?

Useful Expressions

Practice these sentences with apologetic manner.

I am very sorry, but your choice of meal has run out.

Please accept my apologies.

Let me clear this away.

Do you have an on-going flight?

---

33 foreign object : 이물질

Reading

Meal Service

Generally, when you dine in a restaurant, you would be seated at a table and a menu is given. You pre-select your choice form the menu and the restaurant staff will then individually serve you with your orders. The service on board is somewhat different. A menu is extended to every passenger prior to the commencement[34] of the service. This allows passengers to know what they will be served during their journey. Depending on passenger's class of travel, the meal service procedure may differ slightly, from one cabin to another.

In any food service operation, one of the primary objectives is to serve food that is safe, wholesome[35], attractive and nutritive in a clean and safe environment. Hygiene is of paramount importance in any food industry; crew must exercise care in food handling by keeping their hands and nails clean, practice good toilet habits, observe safety precautions[36] and conform[37] to laid down[38] food handling procedures.

---

34 commencement : 개시, 시작
35 wholesome : 건강에 좋은, 위생에 좋은
36 precaution : 조심, 예방조치
37 conform : 따르게 하다, 맞게 하다
38 laid down : 규정대로

D International Departures

In-flight Sales

7

Starter

Put the items for sale into the correct category.

*whisky *eau de toilette *mascara *champagne *lipstick *Ballantine's *bracelet
*make-up remover *pendant *perfume spray *foam cleansing *earrings *scarf
*emulsion *watch *lip balm *Chivas Regal *sun screen *cologne *Mild Seven
*cognac *Godiva *J&B *model aircraft *aftershave *stationary kit *Remy Martin

Perfumes & Cosmetics	Jewelry
Alcohol and tobacco	Gifts

Listening

Listen to the conversation and answer the questions.

1. How much is the perfume? _____ dollars.

2. How much is the wallet? _____ dollars.

3. How does the passenger want to pay? _____

Did You Know

What is the currency in these countries?

China _____   Japan _____   Singapore _____

Hong Kong _____   United Kingdom _____   India _____

France _____   United Arab Emirates _____   Canada _____

Russia _____   Thailand _____   Malaysia _____

---

*JPY (Japanese yen)   *CAD (Canadian dollars)   *CNY (Chinese yuan)   *EUR (Euro)
*AED (Dubai dirhams)   *MYR (Malaysian ringgit)   *SGD (Singapore dollars)
*HKD (Hong Kong dollars)   *THB (Thai baht)   *RUB (Russian ruble)   *INR (Indian rupee)

Vocabulary

Fill blanks with a right word from the box below.

*refund	*purchase	*accept	*currency	*present
*cost	*receipt	*allowance	*change	*charge

1. Would you like to _____ any duty free items?

2. Do you _____ traveler's check?

3. I think you gave me the wrong _____.

4. You should give me $25.

5. The perfume _____s $45.

6. A : I'd like to get a _____ for this I bought on the other flight.
   B : No, problem. May I have your _____, please?

7. Let me check duty free _____ chart.

8. Can you suggest me anything for my daughter's birthday _____?

9. Can I exchange Korean _____ for American dollars?

10. I want to pay with my credit card. Can you _____ me in Singapore dollars?

Conversation 1   *- Would you like to buy any duty free items?*

Listen and practice.

F/A : Would you like to buy any duty free items?

P   : Yes. Can I see a men's wallet?

F/A : Certainly, sir. It's 35 dollars.

P   : Can I pay for this in Thai baht?

F/A : I'm sorry, sir. We don't accept Thai baht.

       We only accept Korean won, US dollars, and Euros.

       We also take major international credit cards.

P   : Okay. I'll pay in Euros. How much is that?

F/A : That will be 29 Euros, sir. Do you need anything else?

P   : No, thank you.

       By the way, do you know how much alcohol I can take into Korea?

F/A : You can take one bottle and here is a duty free allowance chart for

       your reference.

Build-up 1

다음의 우리말을 참고하여 영어로 말해 보세요.

A : 면세품 사시겠습니까?

_____

B : Yes. Can I see men's wallet?

A : 네. 3만원입니다.

_____

B : Can I pay for this in Thai baht?

A : I'm sorry, sir. 저희가 타이바트는 받지 않습니다.

_____

We only accept Korean won, US dollars, and Euros.

주요 국제 신용카드도 받습니다.

_____

B : Okay. I'll pay in Euros. How much is that?

A : 21유로 되겠습니다. 더 필요하신 것 있으세요?

_____

B : No, thank you.

By the way, can I have a glass of water?

A : 물론입니다. 제 동료에게 갖다 드리라 전하겠습니다.

_____

Conversation 2   *- How would you like to pay?*

Listen and practice

F/A : Would you like to order any duty-free items?

P   : Yes, what kinds of whisky do you sell?

F/A : We have Glennfidich, Johnny Walker, Chivas Regal, Ballantine's and
      many more.

      You can refer to the in-flight shopping magazine in your seat pocket, sir.

P   : I see. Do you have anything for ladies?

F/A : Yes, we do have cosmetics, perfumes, watches and jewelry.

P   : Can I have a look at the pearl pendant?

F/A : Sure. We have Mikimoto and Saint-Yves.

P   : All right. I'll take Saint-Yves and a bottle of Ballantine's 17 years.
      How much are they?

F/A : 80 for a pendant plus 58 for a whisky.

      That comes to 138 dollars in total.

      How would you like to pay, sir?

P   : I'll pay in American dollars. Here, 140.

F/A : Thank you, sir. But I'm afraid I don't have any change right now.
      Can I come back with your change
      in a moment?

P   : Okay.

Build-up 2

다음의 우리말을 참고하여 영어로 말해 보세요.

A : 면세품 주문하시겠습니까?

_____

B : Yes, what kinds of perfume do you sell?

A : We have Chanel, Nina Ricci, Kenzo and many more.

　좌석 앞 주머니 안에 있는 기내 판매 안내 책자를 참고하실 수 있습니다.

_____

B : I see. Can you recommend anything for ladies?

A : Yes. What about (name of perfume)?

　상쾌한 향으로 모든 연령층의 여성 손님들에게 인기가 좋습니다.

_____

B : Okay. Keep one for me and can I have a look at the pen?

A : Sure. We have Parker and Waterman.

B : All right. I'll take Parker and a perfume.

　How much are they?

A : 향수는 65달러이고, 펜은 40달러입니다.

_____

　모두 합해서 105달러입니다.

_____

　어떻게 지불하시겠습니까?

_____

B : I'll pay in American dollars. Here you are.

A : Thank you, sir.

Think About

1. What would you do when you have no exact change for him?

>

2. A passenger wants to buy a product that is sold out. What would you do?

>

Useful Expressions

Practice these sentences with smile.

> The neck ties are 70 dollars each.
>
> 38 plus 42 makes 80 dollars.
>
> Four times eight equals 32 dollars.
>
> A hundred dollars minus 75 – that's 25 dollars change.
>
> That comes to 50,000 won.
>
> How would you like to pay?
>
> I will let my colleague know.

Saying Sorry

How many ways can you think of saying 'sorry'?

"Sorry"

_____

_____

_____

_____

If you cannot fulfill a request from a passenger, which of the following might
you include?

✓ an apology

✓ a suggestion as to what the passenger can do so that the request can be granted[39]

✓ an alternative[40] offer

✓ a reassurance[41] that the airline does try to help passenger whenever it can

✓ an explanation of why the request has to be refused

✓ a smile

Here are some useful expressions to use when you cannot fulfill a request:

I'm sorry, sir.

I'm afraid not, ma'am.

Perhaps you would like a _____ instead?

I'm sorry but I'm afraid	we've sold out. we've none left. we don't stock that brand. you can't take that amount into the country.

---

[39] grant : 들어주다, 승인하다
[40] alternative : (둘 중에서 하나를) 택해야 할
[41] reassurance : 안심시킴

D International Departures

Passenger
Requests & Problems

8

Starter

As a flight attendant, you are expected to deal with all sorts of requests and problems.

Make a list of regular, minor passenger requests and problems.

A passenger complains about the cabin temperature.

Listening

Listen to the conversation and answer the questions.

1. Is the passenger's handset broken? _____

2. Does the flight attendant fix the problem? _____

3. How does the flight attendant help the passenger? _____

Did You Know

Complaints are unavoidable. How you handle with determine the final outcome.

Here are 6 simple steps for effective complaints handling.

1. Listen first. Don't interrupt.

2. Accept feelings.

3. Clarify the complaint.

4. Take action immediately.

5. If you can't handle the situation, refer the complaint to someone who can help.

6. Be cheerful and helpful.

Vocabulary

Fill blanks with a right word from the box below.

*adjust	*painkiller	*fever	*airsick	*eyeshades
*souvenir	*decaffeinated	*indigestion	*dizzy	*turbulence

1. Do you have any _____ ? I have a bad headache.

2. I have _____. It seems I ate lunch too fast.

3. Let me _____ cabin temperature.

4. Some people get _____ easily. To them, flying is awful.

5. I am allergic to caffeine. Do you have any _____ hot drink?

6. I feel a bit _____ and short of breath.

7. I'm not feeling well. I think I have a _____.

8. Please fasten your seatbelt. We'll be passing through _____.

9. The light from the window is irritating. Can you get me an _____?

10. You can take this playing card as a _____, if you like.

Conversation 1   *- Please accept my apology.*

Listen and practice.

(A passenger pressed the call button.)

F/A : Excuse me, ma'am. May I help you?

P   : Yes. I told your colleague it was too cold about 15 minutes ago and
       it is still very cold.

F/A : You are right, it is cold.
       I'm afraid it often takes some time for adjusting the temperature.
       I'll get you a blanket, if you'd like.

P   : Yes, please.

F/A : And, would you like some hot drink, ma'am?

P   : That's a good idea. I'll have a cup of tea. Thank you.

Experience our seat

www.thaiair.co.kr

Useful Expressions

Practice these sentences with apologetic manner.

I'm so sorry about that.

That was my mistake. Please forgive me.

I'm afraid we don't have any left.

I know how frustrating it is.

I understand how you feel.

Thank you for understanding.

Build-up 1

Try to solve the passenger's problem and complete the conversation with sentences in the box.

1. F/A : What can I get you, sir?

   P   : A vanilla ice cream, please.

   F/A : Oh, I'm sorry, sir, but _____.

       They've been very popular.

   P   : I don't believe it. You always seem to run out.

   F/A : Once again, _____.

       _____?

   P   : No, thank you.

   F/A : Then, _____?

       We also have some biscuits and sandwiches.

2. P   : Listen! That group of people is making too much noise.

       They are disturbing me.

   F/A : _____.

       I can here how noisy they are and I'm sorry.

       _____.

       If it doesn't get better, then _____.

- I understand, sir.
- We've run out of it.
- Would you like a strawberry ice cream, instead?
- May I offer you something else?
- I'll try to find you another seat.
- I do apologize.
- Let me have a word with them.

Conversation 2 - *Are you allergic to any medicine?*

Listen and practice.

P   : I have a bad headache. Do you have any painkillers?

F/A : I'm sorry to hear that, sir. We have Tylenol on board.

        Are you allergic to any medicine?

P   : No, I'm not.

F/A : All right. I'll get some for you right away.

        (···)

        Here you are. You can take one or two tablets in 8 hours.

        I hope you feel better soon.

        Do you need anything else?

P   : No, thank you. That's all.

F/A : If I were you, I'd get some rest.

(Sometime later)

F/A : Excuse me, sir. How is your headache?

        Are you better now?

P   : Yes, thank you for asking.

F/A : If there is anything I can

        do, please let me know.

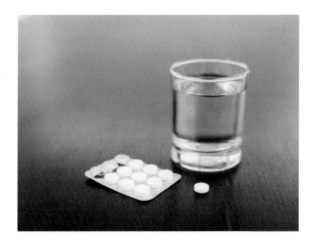

Build-up 2

Complete the conversation with the sentences in the box.

F/A : Excuse me, ma'am. You look pale and shivering.

　　　 _____?

P　 : No, I'm not. I feel really cold and dizzy.

F/A : Okay. Why don't you _____?

　　　 _____?

P　 : No, I don't think so.

F/A : Then, let me get you a blanket.

　　　 How about _____?

P　 : That's a good idea. I'd like hot tea with lemon.

F/A : Certainly, ma'am.

　　　 _____.

(···)

　　　 Here is your tea and blanket.

　　　 We also have _____.

　　　 If you need them, _____.

P　 : Ok, thank you very much.

F/A : Don't mention it, ma'am. _____.

　● some Tylenol and oxygen bottle　　　● having some hot drink
　● I'll come back with your tea and blanket immediately
　● please let me know　　　　　　　　● If I were you, I'd get some rest, too
　● Are you feeling alright　　　　　　● recline and seat back
　● Do you have any fever?

100 English for Flight Attendants

Think About

1. What would you do if a passenger complains about an earache?

2. What would you do if a passenger faints?

Useful Expressions

Practice these sentences.

How are you feeling?

Do you have any pain?

Where is the pain?

Do you have any allergies to any medicine?

We have Tylenol. Would that be alright?

I'm here to help you.

Reading

What Passengers Say?

These are complains of airline passengers. Read them and discuss how you would treat passengers with different manner.

"I ordered an Asian vegetarian meal through my travel agent two weeks before my flight. I even called your Frankfurt office on the day of my departure to confirm my request, and was assured it would be seen to. However, no such meal was catered! I received lots of polite apologies from the cabin crew and a "make-believe" version of a vegetarian meal was prepared. I was upset and very disappointed that your airline allows such an incident to occur."

"The dinner menu offered a choice of fish or duck for the main course, but when it came to my turn, I was told there was no more duck left. As I was very hungry I ate the fish. However, I saw another stewardess on the other side still serve duck to her passengers. I became annoyed because she could, and should, have taken a few seconds to find out whether my preferred choice was still available in the first place."

"My 19 month old son took ill enroute to Perth. I called for assistance as my son was vomiting continuously. To my astonishment they ignored all effort to help us. The sight was obviously too horrifying for your staff to look at, much less if I needed assistance."

D International Departures

Preparing for
Landing

9

What do cabin crew need to do before landing?

Listening

Listen to the captain's announcement and answer the questions.

1. What time does the plane land in New York? _____

2. How is the weather in New York? _____

Did You Know

Who is the longest serving flight attendant?

Jamie Schwaberow for The New York Times

Ron Akana, the 83-year old flight attendant to enter the Guinness Records. 83-year old Ron Akana had joined the United Airlines in 1949 when still a student at the University of Hawaii and, has been working as a flight attendant with UA since then. He was one of the first male flight attendants of the airline and had been one for 63-years. That long tenure[42] in the air has now earned him recognition from the Guinness Book of World Records as the longest serving flight attendant and they have confirmed that his name would be entered in its pages in the October-2012 edition.

---

42 tenure : 재직권, 보유 기간

Vocabulary

Fill blanks with a right word from the box below.

*switch	*expect	*secure	*comply with	*disembarkation
*emergency	*resident	*final	*strap in	*difference

1. Have you filled in your _____ card, sir?

2. Sir, the captain has _____ed on the seat belt sign.

3. This is the _____ exit door. You will have to remove your bag.

4. We are _____ing turbulence.

5. Everyone must return to their seats and _____.

6. Flight attendants must ensure that all passengers _____ airline regulations.

7. Have you done your _____ checks for landing?

8. I _____ d the trolley in the galley.

9. Is there any time _____ between Seoul and New York?

10. If you are a _____, then you don't need to fill in this form.

Conversation 1   - Would you like me to help?

Listen and practice.

P : Excuse me. Do I need any form to enter the states?

F/A : Are you a U.S. citizen or a resident?

P : No, I'm an Australian.

F/A : Are you visiting or immigrating?

P : I'm just visiting.

F/A : Then, please fill out these forms.

   One is for the immigration and the other one is for the customs.

   Would you like me to help you?

P : No, I can manage. Thank you.

Build-up 1

Complete the conversation with your own answer.

1. **P** : I'll be staying in Korea for two weeks.

   Do I need to fill out immigration card?

   F/A : _____

2. **P** : I am transiting at Incheon and continuing on to Shanghai.

   Do I still need to fill out immigration form?

   F/A : _____

3. **P** : I am transiting without visa.

   Do I need to fill out this card?

   F/A : Are you leaving the airport?

   P : Yes, I'll be staying at Asea Hotel.

   F/A : Then, _____

Did You Know

TWOV (Travel Without Visa) is the program which allows certain foreign nationals to transit without visa if they meet these requirements:

   ✓ They are from certain countries;

   ✓ They hold a valid passport and

   ✓ They travel on an approved airline.

Conversation 2 — *We've closed the bar for landing.*

Listen and practice.

F/A : Excuse me, sir.

Would you mind keeping your bag under the seat for landing?

P : OK.

F/A : Thank you, sir.

And may I collect your headphones?

P : Here you are.

By the way, could I have another cocktail?

F/A : I'm sorry, sir. We've closed the bar for landing

We will be landing in 15 minutes.

Can I get you something else?

P : No, thank you.

Build-up 2

다음의 우리말을 참고하여 영어로 말해 보세요.

A : Excuse me, sir.

착륙을 위해 가방을 머리 위 선반에 보관해 주시겠습니까?

_____

B : OK.

A : Thank you, sir.

빈 잔을 치워드릴까요?

_____

B : Here you are.

By the way, could I buy a bottle of Scotch whisky?

A : I'm sorry, sir.

착륙 준비로 더 이상 기내판매를 하지 않습니다.

_____

약 10분 후에 착륙할 것입니다.

_____

원하신다면 돌아오는 비행편에 상품을 받으실 수 있도록 사전주문 예약[43]을 해드릴까요?

_____

B : Oh, that will be great. How can I order?

A : 좌석 앞 주머니 속에 있는 사전주문 신청서[44]를 작성하셔서 저희에게 건네 주십시오.

_____

---

43 사전주문 예약 : pre-order service
44 사전주문 신청서 : pre-order form

Think About

1. Captain has announced half an hour delay of the flight due to heavy traffic at the airport. What would you do if passengers are complaining about it?

2. A passenger wants to go to the toilet after the captain has made the final announcement. What would you say and do?

Useful Expression

I do understand sir/ma'am.

We will try our best.

I will keep you informed.

We'll get you off the plane as fast as possible.

Please go back to your seat and fasten your seatbelt.

Reading

All Nippon Airways to Supply IPads to Cabin Attendant
(9/27/2011)

In what it says is a world first, All Nippon Airways plans to equip its 6,000 cabin attendants with iPads "to provide a better service to passengers and improve business efficiency," the company said in a statement.

The iPads would take the place of paper training manuals and give the attendants constant access to the latest information, the statement said.

A.N.A. expected the digital manual would boost[45] productivity[46] by the equivalent[47] of around 100 cabin attendants per year.

---

45 boost : 밀어올림, 상승
46 productivity : 생산성
47 equivalent : 상당하는, 맞먹는

British Airways to Start Flights between London and Seoul

(5/8/2012)

British Airways will begin flights between Heathrow Airport, serving London, and Incheon Airport, serving Seoul, with services six times a week set to start Dec. 2, 2012.

The nonstop route will be served by Boeing 777-200ER aircraft outfitted[48] with four cabins - first class and business class, with seats that turn into beds, premium economy and economy class.

British Airways will be the only member of the Oneworld alliance[49] to serve the route.

기사 출처 : From *International Traveler*, International Herald Tribune

---

[48] outfitted : 장착된
[49] alliance : 동맹

International Departures

D

Landing & Farewell

10

Starter

File: Stornoway Airport Runway.jpg/ From Wikipedia, the free encyclopedia

1. Why is it important to smile and say goodbye to passengers?

2. What do flight attendants do after the flight?

Listening

Listen to the in-flight purser's announcement and answer the questions.

1. Why has the flight been delayed? _____

2. How did the purser end her announcement? _____

Vocabulary

Listen to the final announcement again and fill in the missing words.

Ladies and gentlemen, _____ to New York. The _____ is 9:30 in the morning, Tuesday, October, 17th and the _____ is 15 degrees Celsius or 59 degrees Fahrenheit. Today, we are _____ due to heavy traffic _____ at the airport. We _____ your patience and kind understanding.

For your safety, please _____ seated until the seat belt sign is off and leave all your hand-luggage safely stowed.

Before you _____ the aircraft, please _____ that you have all your personal _____ with you and be careful when opening overhead bins as items may fall out.

We wish you a _____ stay and we hope to see you again soon. Thank you and good bye.

Did You Know

From time to time we have dignitaries[50] traveling on our flight. They could be Royalties, Government Heads of State, Presidents, Ministers of Foreign Countries, etc. It is only right that we know how to address the dignitaries by their proper title.

Passenger's Designation	Refer to Passenger As
H. M. The King	Your Majesty
H. M. The Queen	Your Majesty
Duke[51] or Duchess	Your Grace
Earl[52], Viscount[53], Lord[54], Baron[55]	Your Grace
Count, Ambassador	Your Excellency
The President	Mr. President
Prime Minister	Mr. Prime Minister
The Pope[56]	Your Holiness
Priest	Reverend Father
Nun	Sister

---

[50] dignitary : 고위인사
[51] duke : 공작
[52] earl : 백작 (= count)
[53] viscount : 자작
[54] lord : 영주, 귀족
[55] baron : 남작
[56] pope : 교황

Conversation 1   - *Just stay in your seat for a little.*

Listen and practice.

F/A : Excuse me, Mr. Smith.

Your wheelchair will be ready after all the passengers disembark.

Would you mind staying in your seat until the wheelchairs arrive?

P   : Sure. No problem.

F/A : Thank you for your understanding, Mr. Smith.

Is there any baggage I can help you with?

P   : Yes, there is one suit case in the overhead bin.

F/A : All right. Just stay in your seat for a little bit.

Our ground staff will come and take you to the airport.

P   : Okay. Thank you very much.

F/A : Don't mention it, sir.

Build-up 1

다음의 우리말을 참고하여 영어로 말해 보세요.

A : Excuse me, Mr. Smith.

다른 승객들이 내리신 후에 손님의 휠체어를 준비해 드리겠습니다.

_____

휠체어가 도착할 때까지 자리에서 기다려주시겠습니까?

_____

B : Sure. No problem.

A : 이해해 주셔서 감사합니다.

_____

제가 들어드릴 짐이 있으신가요?

_____

B : Yes, there is one suit case on the overhead bin.

A : All right. 잠시만 더 좌석에서 기다려 주십시오.

_____

저희 지상직원이 손님을 공항까지 모셔다 드릴겁니다.

_____

B : Okay. Thank you very much.

A : Don't mention it, sir.

Think About

1. How would you help for a mother traveling with infant to disembark?

2. What would you say to passengers when it is very cold outside?

3. What would you do if you find someone's belongings after all the passengers disembarked?

Useful Expressions

Practice these sentences.

> I suggest that you stay here for a few minutes.
>
> I suggest that you have your coats ready.
>
> Please watch your step. It is slippery.
>
> I suggest that you fill out the immigration form before you disembark.

Conversation 2

Listen and practice.

O : Officer   P : Passenger

O : Good morning. Your passport and arrival form, please.

P : Here you are.

O : What is the purpose of your visit?

P : I'm here for the holidays.

O : I see. How long are you going to stay in the United States?

P : About 2 weeks.

O : Where will you be staying?

P : I'm going to stay at my sister's home in Astoria.

O : Good. Here is your passport. Enjoy your stay.

P : Thank you.

ⒷBuild-up 2

다음의 우리말을 참고하여 영어로 말해 보세요.

A : Good morning. May I see your customs declaration form?
B : 네. 여기 있습니다.

A : Do you have anything to declare?
B : 아니오, 개인용품들 뿐입니다.

A : I see. Can you open your suitcase?
B : 물론입니다. 제가 열겠습니다.

A : What is this?
B : 제 언니에게 줄 선물입니다.

A : How much does it cost?
B : 한국에서 샀는데, 30달러 정도입니다.

A : Okay. That's it. You may proceed.
B : Thank you.

⒰seful Expression

I only have my personal effects.

They are only my personal effects.

Let me open it.

Try This!

Saying About Korea

Foreign passengers may often ask you about Korea. How much do you know about Korea? Try these quizzes.

1. Describe the Korean flag.

_____

_____

2. What is the population of Korea?

_____

_____

3. What is the approximate taxi fare from Incheon International Airport to Seoul City Hall?

_____

_____

4. What are the following places famous for?

- Insa-dong _____
- Gyeongbok Palace _____
- Busan _____
- Jeju island _____
- Gangnam _____
- Folk Village _____
- Everland _____

5. Which of these words are not used to describe Korea?

*dynamic	*crowded	*clean	*tropical	*fashion-conscious
*rich	*expensive	*fun	*surprising	*kingdom *exciting

6. Can you add more which you think would be appropriate?

```
```

D International Departures

In-flight
Announcement

11

1. What is the purpose of the in-flight announcement?

2. Why is the in-flight announcement important?

3. What makes good in-flight announcement?

영어 방송 연습

외국어로 방송할 때에는 그 나라말에 적합한 자연스러운 목소리, 정확한 발음과 억양을 구사하도록 노력한다. 또한 방송문을 유창하게 읽을 수 있도록 평소에 많은 노력을 기울이고, 밝고 경쾌한 톤을 유지하기 위하여 밝은 미소를 띠고 방송한다.

1. 발음 연습

1) 장모음(Long vowels) vs. 단모음(short vowels)

eat	it
read	rid
piece	piss
green	grin
peel	pill
pool	pull
seat	sit

 Exercise

a) If you eat that pill, it might make you sick.

b) If you eat that peel, it might make you sick.

2) /r/ vs. /l/

read	lead
race	lace
rim	limb
crime	climb
fire	file
war	wall

Exercise

a) The doctor is going to collect the papers.

b) The doctor is going to correct the papers.

3) /f/ vs. /p/

file	pile
fin	pin
face	pace
chief	cheap
leaf	leap
wife	wipe

 Exercise

a) The chief asked for a cheap price.

b) They made the files piled.

4) /b/ vs. /v/

ban	van
berry	very
boat	vote
curb	curve
lobes	loaves
robe	rove

 Exercise

a) I only want the best.

b) I only want the vest.

5) /d/ vs. /ð/

dan	than
dare	their
wordy	worthy
breeding	breathing
bade	bathe

 Exercise

a) Do you think the day will come soon?

b) Do you think they will come soon?

6) /s/ vs. /θ/

sank	thank
saw	thaw
face	faith
bass	bath
tense	tenth

 Exercise

a) Can you see the moss?

b) Can you see the moth?

7) 어말 파열음 (Final plosives)

Say these sentences. What is the difference?

Give her back to them!

Give her bag to them!

영어의 파열음은 모두 자음 발음이며, 단어의 끝에 오는 /p, b, t, d, k, g/ 자음을 어말 파열음 (final plosive)라고 한다. 명확하고 세련된 발음을 하기 위해서는 단어 끝에 오는 파열음을 의식하고 발음해야 한다.

rip	rib
cup	cub
kit	kid
bought	board
lock	log
leak	league

 Exercise

a) You are now allowed to use your electronic devices.

b) For details, you can find Asea in-flight magazine in your seat pocket.

2. 끊어 읽기(Pause)

Tom said, "Bill broke the window."
"Tom," said Bill, "broke the window."

아버지 가죽을 먹는다.
아버지가 죽을 먹는다.

위의 문장처럼 제대로 끊어 읽지 않으면 문장의 의미가 완전히 바뀌어 버린다. 엉뚱한 끊어 읽기, 리듬, 억양 등은 의미 자체를 바꾸어 버릴 수 있기 때문에 올바른 끊어 읽기는 상당히 중요하다.

● 의미 단위로 끊어 읽기 요령

1) 문장 부호들을 주목한다

쉼표 (comma), 마침표 (period) 등의 문장 부호는 의미 덩어리를 표시한다. 문장 안에서 이런 문장 부호를 만나면 그곳에서 잠시 끊어서 읽는다.

Ladies and gentlemen, for your safety, please return to your seat, and fasten your seat belt.

2) 주어가 긴 경우 주어 다음, 접속사나 관계사 앞에서 끊어 읽는다

 Exercise

다음 문장들을 적당한 위치에서 끊어 읽어 보세요.

① All passengers entering into Korea are requested to have your entry documents ready.

② At this time, we request that you return to your seat and fasten your seatbelt.

3. 강세(Word Stress)와 음절(Syllable)

강세란 2음절 이상의 단어에서 한 부분을 다른 부분보다 강하게 발성하는 것을 말한다. 영어에서는 같은 단어라도 강세의 위치에 따라 의미가 달라지기도 한다(예 : object[óbdʒikt] 물건, 물체 / object[əbdʒékt] 반대하다, 항의하다).

음절은 자음과 모음으로 구성된 발음의 최소 단위이다. 영어는 모음을 기준으로 음절이 나뉘어지는데, 한국어와 영어 발음의 음절이 다르다는 것을 이해하는 것이 중요하다. 한국인의 영어 발음이 어색한 이유 중에 하나가 바로 한국어와 영어의 음절이 다르기 때문이다. straight라는 단어를 한글로 표기하면 '스트레이트'가 되어 5음절이지만, 영어는 1음절로 발음된다. 즉, 영어 단어를 한국어 표기처럼 읽어서는 영어가 아니라는 사실을 이해하고 발음을 처음 배울 때 잘 따라하는 것이 좋다.

Exercise

다음의 단어들의 올바른 강세를 표시하고, 음절 수를 세어 보세요.

강세 표시	음절 수
flight	
bassinet	
safety	
drinks	
San Francisco	

4. 리듬과 억양(Rhythm and Intonation)

리듬은 소리의 세고 약함(강약)과 길고 짧음(장단)이 어울려 나타나는 소리 흐름의 패턴을 말한다.

각 음절을 거의 똑같은 길이와 강도로 발음하며 강약의 변화가 많지 않은 한국어와 달리 영어는 강세에 의하여 박자가 맞추어지고, 문장 속에서 개별 단어의 강세가 이어지면서 리듬이 생기는 강세와 리듬이 중요한 언어이다. 영어에서 의미 전달을 잘 하기 위해서는 내용어 (content words : 명사, 동사, 형용사, 부사, 의문사, 부정어 등)를 강조하고 기능어 (function words : 관사, 인칭 대명사, 접속사, 전치사, be동사, 조동사 등)는 약하게 발음 해야 한다.

Exercise

다음 문장에서 내용어와 기능어를 찾아보고, 내용어는 강하게, 기능어는 약하게 발음하여 읽어 보세요.

① The people should have enjoyed the books.

② They will have to stay up late if they are going to finish their homework.

억양은 그 문장의 종류, 즉 평서문, 의문문, 명령문, 감탄문 등에 따라 올림조, 내림조, 올림내림 혼합조 등으로 소리의 올라감과 내려감으로 구분한다.

Exercise

다음 문장을 내용에 따라 알맞은 억양으로 읽어 보세요.

① What a wonderful day!

② Did you see her?

③ We have landed at Los Angeles International Airport.

5. 연음(Liaison/Linking sound)

연음이란 앞 단어 끝의 자음과 뒤에 오는 단어의 약모음이 연결될 때 마치 한 단어처럼 발음되는 경우를 말한다. 영어 방송을 할 때에는 연음을 중심으로 생략(deletion: 음이 약하게 또는 아예 생략되어 발음됨), 동화(assimilation: 두 개의 음이 비슷한 소리가 되는 현상) 등의 영어 특유의 발음 현상을 제대로 처리하며 낭독할 수 있어야 한다.

1) 자음 다음에 오는 모음을 연결하여 한 단어처럼 읽는다

예) welcome aboard, take off, switched on, in front of, that your, turned off, provide you, fill out, get along, glad to

2) 연속된 자음일 경우 한쪽 자음이 탈락한다

예) bus stop, next time, get together, please stop

6. 표현과 성량(Expression and Volume)

기내 방송은 문어체적인 표현보다는 구어체적인 표현으로 해야 자연스럽고 단순히 정보를 전달한다는 느낌보다는 승객 한 분, 한 분께 정성을 다하여 다정하고 친근감 있는 목소리로 상냥하게 설명한다는 느낌이 들도록 방송해야 한다.

또한, 마이크는 비행 전 반드시 테스트 방송을 실시하여 볼륨이나 잡음 발생 여부 등을 미리 파악하고, 자신의 목소리와 조화를 이룰 수 있도록 해야 한다.

Exercise

다음 문장을 감정을 넣어 승객께 말하듯이 읽어 보세요.

① Good morning, ladies and gentlemen. Welcome aboard flight AS 432 to Bangkok.

② We sincerely apologize for any inconvenience caused.

7. 비행 편수(Flight No.) 읽는 법

영어로 비행 편수를 읽을 때는 숫자를 한자리 단위로 끊어서 읽으며, '0'은 zero로 읽는다. 단, 0이 중간에 있는 편수는 O/ou/로 읽어도 무방하다.

예) 123편: ONE TWO THREE

701편: SEVEN ZERO ONE / SEVEN O ONE

016편: _____

8. 영어 시간 읽는 법

영어로 시간을 읽을 때는 시간과 분을 구분한다. 오전은 in the morning, 오후는 in the evening으로 읽고, 12시를 제외한 매시 정각은 o'clock을 삽입하여 읽는다. 1분부터 9분까지는 'O/ou/'를 중간에 넣어 읽는다.

예) 밤 12:00 twelve midnight

밤 12:01 twelve O one in the morning

낮 12:00 twelve noon

낮 12:05 twelve O five in the afternoon

오전 2:00 _____

오후 4:00 _____

오후 5:15 _____

오전 7:08 _____

기내 방송 연습

1. Welcome

Good morning, ladies and gentlemen.

On behalf of Asea Airlines, welcome aboard our flight AS 012 to New York.

Captain Kim is in command and your in-flight manager is Ms. Choi.

Our flight time to New York will be 13 hours and 10 minutes.

Before we take off, please make sure that your seatback is upright, and secure your tray table.

Please fasten your seat belt and observe the "No smoking' sign.

Portable electronic devices including hand phones and smart phones can interfere with navigation equipment on board.

Please make sure they are turned off during take-off and landing.

We're glad to have you with us, and we wish you a pleasant flight.

2. After Take-off

Ladies and gentlemen,

The seat belt sign is now off.

In case of any unexpected turbulence, we strongly recommend you keep your seat belt fastened at all times while seated.

When you open the overhead compartment, be careful as the contents may fall out.

You may now use portable electronic devices.

Please make sure that you switch your hand phones and smart phones to the airplane mode.

For more information about services available on this flight, please refer to the in-flight magazine in your seat pocket.

Thank you.

3. Duty Free Sales

Ladies and gentlemen,

In a few minutes, we'll begin our in-flight duty free sales.

If you'd like to purchase any items, please let us know as the duty free sales cart passes by your seat.

We'd like to remind you that the duty free allowance for the United States is one bottle of liquor and one carton of cigarettes.

For more information, please refer to the in-flight shopping magazine in your seat pocket.

If you need any assistance, our cabin crew is happy to help you.

Thank you.

4. Entry Documents: Korea

Ladies and gentlemen,

Our cabin crew will be handing out entry documents for entering into Korea.

Non Korean citizens must complete both an Arrival card and Customs form.

Only one customs form is required per family.

Today's date is July 1st, and this is Asea Airlines flight AS 011.

Please notify cabin crew if you need any information or assistance.

We will be happy to assist you.

Thank you.

5. Arrival Information: Korea

Ladies and gentlemen,

For entering Korea, please have your passport and other entry documents ready.

If you're carrying foreign currency more than 10,000 US dollars, or if you acquired more than 400 US dollars worth of articles abroad, please declare them on the customs form.

If you're carrying any kind of fruit, plant or meat products, they must be declared on the customs form and be quarantined.

For further details, please contact a flight attendant.

Thank you.

6. Turbulence

Ladies and gentlemen,

Due to turbulent weather, please return to your seat and fasten your seat belt.
Also we must suspend cabin service until conditions improve. Thank you for
your understanding.

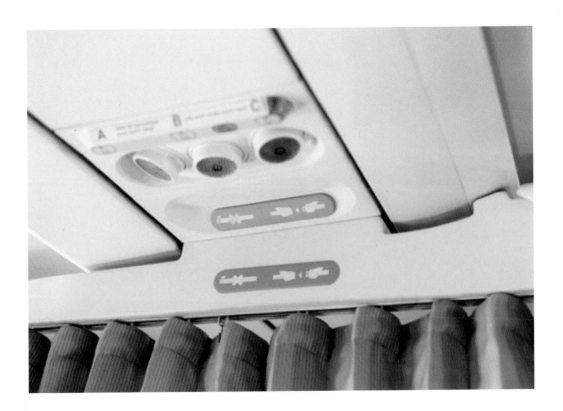

7. Headphone Collection

Ladies and gentlemen,

We hope you have enjoyed our entertainment program.

Our flight attendants will collect your headphones shortly.

Your cooperation is much appreciated.

8. Approaching

Ladies and gentlemen,

We are approaching John F. Kennedy International Airport, New York.

Please store your carry-on items in the overhead bins or under the seat in front of you.

Thank you for your cooperation.

9. Landing

Ladies and gentlemen,

We will be landing shortly.

In preparation for landing, please fasten your seat belt, return your seatback and tray table to the upright position, and open your window shades.

Also, please discontinue the use of electronic devices until the aircraft has been parked at the gate.

Thank you.

10. Farewell at Terminating Station

Ladies and gentlemen, welcome to New York.

We have just landed at John F Kennedy International Airport.

The local time is now 10:05 in the morning, on Monday, July 2nd, and the temperature is 18 degrees Celsius or 64 degrees Fahrenheit.

For your safety, remain seated with the seatbelt fastened until the aircraft has come to a complete stop and the seatbelt sign is switched off.

For those of you who would like to use your mobile phone, it is safe to do so now.

Before leaving the aircraft make sure you take all your belongings with you. If you are transferring to another flight and need assistance contact the Airport Service staff.

We would like to thank you for choosing Asea Airlines.

We hope that you have enjoyed your flight, and look forward to seeing you again soon.

D International Departures

Getting a Job

12

Calling Cabin Crew.
Join one of the world's youngest fleet.

Being a cabin crew, is it a good career?

Did You Know

A cabin crew job attracts thousands of applicants throughout the world. You will be competing among the best candidates. Most people have impression that by having good looks (though it is a plus point), you will definitely get the job. However, when airlines recruit, they are looking for someone who can embrace and propel the cooperate image of their airline. You need to be a good communicator and a good team player. You must know how to take good care of yourself and you must be presentable.

www.philippineairlines.com

Think About

What questions do you think the interviews ask? List them.

1. _____

2. _____

3. _____

4. _____

5. _____

6. _____

7. _____

8. _____

9. _____

10. _____

Things to Remember

✓ Types of English Interview

1. Interview with Korean interviewer (내국인 영어 면접)

2. Interview with native speakers (외국인 영어 면접)

3. Personal interview (개별 면접)

4. Group interview (그룹 면접)

5. Team assessment (팀 평가 면접)

6. Group discussion (그룹 토론)

7. Role play (역할극)

✓ How to Prepare

1. Research applying airlines.

2. Be familiar with aviation knowledge.

3. Know yourself.

4. Practice makes perfect.

5. Study with peers.

6. Practice answering a lot of different questions naturally.

✓ Interview Day Tips

1. Be honest and open.

2. Be positive and show your interest.

3. Keep your sense of humor and show your smile consistently.

4. Don't prepare a long speech.

5. Don't be nervous.

6. Prepare your own questions about the company.

Exercise

Refer to the following answers and make your own statement.

1. Greeting (인사하기)

Q1. How are you?

How do you do?

How are you doing?

How are you feeling today?

How are things going?

A1. I'm pretty good, thank you.

I'm fine but a little nervous.

I'm pleased to be here.

첫인상의 중요성은 아무리 강조해도 지나치지 않을 것이다. 하지만 대부분의 지원자들이 면접실에 들어서면서 면접관과 눈이 마주치면 당황하고 만다. 긴장을 풀고 자신감 있게 인사하자.

Q2. Please introduce yourself.

Tell me about yourself.

Would you like to introduce yourself?

A2. Certainly, sir.

I am Lee Daehan who is applying for a flight attendant position.

I am Kim Yujin majoring in Aircraft Cabin Service Management with a first aid certificate.

---

2. Personal Information (개인 신상에 관한 질문)

Q1. When were you born?

A1. I was born on the 24th of November, 1992.

Q2. How many people are there in your family?
Can you tell me about your family?

A2. There are five of us in my family. My parents, an elder sister, a younger brother and me.

My father is an accountant, and my mother is a teacher. My sister is working as a nurse and my brother is serving army.

Q3. How is your heath?
Are you in good health?

A3. I am in good health. I haven't even been sick since high school. I have no health problems. I usually exercise and eat well.

Q4. What is your personality like?
What would you say about your personality?
What do you think of yourself?

A4. I am prudent.

I am responsible.

I like to help those in need.

I like to be around people.

I consider myself flexible.

I have a sense of humor. My friends tell me that I'm funny and entertaining.

성격을 나타내는 형용사

passionate	열정적인	warm	따뜻한
objective	객관적인	adventurous	모험심 강한
humble	겸손한	sensible	분별력 있는
diligent	부지런한	sociable	사교적인
strong-willed	의지가 강한	productive	생산적인
sincere	성실한, 진실한	trustworthy	믿을 수 있는
outgoing	외향적인	compassionate	인정 많은
bold	대범한, 배짱 있는	conservative	보수적인
easygoing	수더분한	dedicated	헌신적인
stubborn	고집 센, 완고한	thoughtful	사려 깊은

▶ Can you think of any other words that represent you?

Q5. What are your strengths?

What are you good at?

A5. I am strong-willed. I have been studying Chinese for myself during college days. Now I have not much difficulty of speaking Chinese so I enjoyed my trip to China last summer.

My key strength is interpersonal skills. My friends tell me that I am kind and understanding.

특별한 기술이나 능력을 나타내는 표현

adaptability	적응력	problem-solving skills	문제해결능력
leadership	리더쉽	time management	시간관리 능력
negotiation skills	협상기술	ability to focus	집중력
flexibility	융통성	risk management	위기관리 능력
communication skills	의사소통 능력	independent	독립적인

Q6. What are your hobbies?

What do you do in your free time?

What do you do for fun?

How do you spend your free time?

A6. I usually go to the gym for a workout. It helps me in shape, too.

I spend my free time volunteering.

I enjoy spending time with my friends in my free time. It's a great way to unwind.

면접에서 취미에 대해 이야기 할 때에는 단순한 취미에 그치는 것이 아니라 취미를 통해 자기개발에 힘쓰고 있다는 사실을 드러내도록 한다.

3. School Life (학창 시절)

Q1. Tell me about your school days.

Tell me a little about your college life.

How was your school life?

A1. I really enjoyed my school life. I learned customer service skills and foreign languages from my major.

I had various experiences during college days. I was a member of volunteer club and student council. These activities taught me how to get along well with others.

My college days have been very busy but really fun. It helped me to shape my life.

_____

_____

Q2. What was your major?

What did you learn from your major?

Why did you choose your major?

A2. I really wanted to be a flight attendant, so I decided to major in Aircraft Cabin Service Management.

I wanted to work right after I graduate from college, so I decided to choose pragmatic studies.

I managed to learn foreign languages, customer service, aircraft safety equipment and procedures, tourism management, and etc.

_____

_____

학업 관련 단어

major	전공	minor	부전공
required courses	필수 과목	elective courses	선택 과목
freshman	1학년	sophomore	2학년
junior	3학년	senior	4학년
graduate school	대학원	bachelor's degree	학사 학위
master's degree	석사 학위	Ph.D.	박사 학위

대학 시절의 경험과 관련한 단어들

club activity	동아리 활동	MT(membership training)	엠티
festival	축제	fund-raising	기금 모금
volunteer club	봉사 동아리	student council	학생회
student representative	학생 대표	president	회장

4. Job Experience (업무 경험)

Q1. Did you have any part-time experience?

Did you work during college?

Tell me about your job experience.

A1. I was an intern at Asea hotel during summer vacation. My internship experience has prepared me to work with various people. I learned a hard lesson dealing with all sorts of people.

I had a part-time job at a restaurant for a year. I learned customer service and patience there.

_____

_____

_____

아르바이트 업무

tutoring	과외	baby-sit	아기 돌보기
customer service	고객 서비스	cashier	계산원
receptionist	안내	serving customers	서빙

훌륭한 직장에서 일한 경험 뿐만 아니라 본인이 가진 작은 경험이라도 적극적으로 알리도록 노력한다. 본인이 생각하기에 별볼일 없는 아르바이트라 할지라도 단순한 업무를 통해 큰 깨달음을 얻었거나 직업 의식을 느끼는 지원자는 더 좋은 점수를 받는다.

Q2. What did you do with the money you earned?

A2. I earned 800,000 won for 2-month internship program and I spent the money for my college tuition.

I didn't get paid much but I give it to my parents.

_____

_____

5. About the Company (지원한 회사와 지원 동기에 대한 질문)

Q1. Tell me what you know about our airline.
Do you know anything about our company?
What do you know about our company?

A1. Asea Airlines was founded on September, 1990 and the President is Kim Jihoon at the moment. Asea Airlines is one of the largest flag carrier in Korea and it operates international services to 42 cities in 20 countries throughout the world. It has rapidly expanded its operating services and is known for its high quality service. I think Asea Airlines is one of the world's greatest airlines in the world.

_____

_____

_____

Q2. Have you ever flown with our airlines?

A2. Yes, I used Asea Airlines when I took a school trip to Jeju in high school. It was a pleasant experience.
No, unfortunately, I've never been on Asea Airlines. But I've heard its in-flight service is great and I really want to be on board as a flight attendant not just as a passenger.

_____

_____

Q3. What do you think about our uniform?

A3. I think it is very sophisticated and pretty.

The uniform is extremely beautiful. It looks refined.

I like your company's uniform very much. It presents the image of Korea.

Q4. Do you know the new cities that we have recently started serving?

A4. Yes, I read that Asea Airlines now flies to Bali in Indonesia. I think it attracts more honeymooners.

평소 기내 잡지 및 마일리지 프로그램, 신규 취항 노선 등을 숙지하여 최대한 성실하고 상세하게 답변한다. 지원하는 회사에 대한 관심이 많고 관련 지식이 풍부하다는 인상을 전달해야 한다. 만약 질문하는 내용에 대해 모른다면 어설픈 답변보다는 솔직하게 모른다고 대답하는 것이 낫다.

Q5. Why did you apply for this company?

What makes you to apply for our company?

A5. Your airline is the best company in the aviation industry. My goal is to work with the best.

I am impressed with the fact that Asea airlines has been expanding successfully. That is amazing.

Flight attendants should be flexible to adjust to new environment and people.

My study and experience in college will be a great asset of your company.

회사 지원 동기를 설명할 때는 그 기업의 비전 및 경영 철학, 기업 문화 등에 대해 미리 숙지하여 회사의 긍정적인 면을 부각하는 내용을 언급하도록 한다. 지원동기는 자기소개와 더불어 면접에서 가장 많이 물어보는 내용이므로, 남들이 다같이 대답하는 평범한 내용보다는 본인의 어떠한 점이 회사에 이익을 줄 수 있는지 충분히 고민해 보자.

Q6. Why do you want to be a flight attendant?

Why do you apply for this position?

A6. It is my dream to be a flight attendant since very young. It is my dream to realize my goals in your company.

I've always wanted to be a flight attendant since I was a little girl. And I think working as a flight attendant would give me the best opportunity to use the knowledge I've studied in college.

_____

_____

_____

6. Personal Opinion (자신의 의견 말하기)

Q1. Which one is more important, safety or good service?

A1. They are both important; however, I should put safety before good service. It is the duty of the flight attendants to ensure the passengers' safety.

Q2. Do you prefer working with others or by yourself?
Do you prefer to work individually or on a team?

A2. I prefer to work with others. Working in a team is more fun and better. I am certain that team players get things done faster.

Q3. What is your goal in 5 years?
Where do you see yourself in 5 years?

A3. In five years, I can see myself as an assistant purser at Asea Airlines. I am sure that my major in college help me perform better as a flight attendant.

입사 면접 단골 질문이다. 평소에 5년 이내의 단기 목표와 10년 후의 장기 목표를 설정하여 지원하는 분야나 회사에서의 목표를 준비한다.

Q4. Have you applied for any other airlines?

A4. No, I haven't. This is my first interview. I am so delighted to be here. Yes, I have applied for Korea Airline before. I did not achieve a good result, but now I have a better opportunity applying for Asea Airlines.

_____

_____

Q5. If you are failed this time, what would you do from now?

A5. I really don't want to imagine that. But if I'm unsuccessful in this interview, I will try hard to find out what my weak points are and prepare for the next interview.

_____

_____

7. Saying Goodbye (끝인사)

I1. Okay. That was the last question. Thank you.

A1. Thank you, sir. I've enjoyed talking with you.

I2. That's the end of the interview. We will let you know the result as soon as possible.

A2. I appreciate your time, sir. I hope to see you again.

마지막 질문에 답변을 마쳤다고 해서 면접이 끝난 것이 아니다. 면접 장소를 나가기 전, 반드시 면접관에게 시간을 내 준 것에 대한 감사의 인사를 전한다. 면접관에게 기억에 남을 만한 인상을 줄 수 있도록 자신이 지원하고자 하는 분야에 대한 간단한 질문을 준비하는 것도 좋다.

D International Departures

Appendix

[Appendix 1]

1. Listening Script

Chapter 01

Listening

F : I started as a flight attendant 2 years ago. I finished my training and my main responsibility is passenger safety. I also look after passenger's comfort. Communication between crew is very important. I report to the purser what happens in the cabin. I enjoy international flights and working with different people. I love to travel and see new places. However, it is a hard job. It is not easy to live a normal life. I have to work long hours and serve demanding passengers.

Chapter 03

Listening

F : Good afternoon, everyone. My name is Min Hee Lee, your purser today. Welcome to AS 012 to New York. I'd like to share with you some flight information. The scheduled departure time is 09:00 and we expect to arrive at 12:30 local time. We are expecting 5 passengers in First class, 80 in Business and 296 in Economy. Have you all checked your duty? ⋯ Good. Also check that your passport and visa is valid. Be sure to wear your ID all the time.

Chapter 04

Listening

M : Good morning. Welcome aboard, ma'am. May I see your boarding pass?

F : Here you are.

M : Thank you, ma'am. Your seat is 31A window.

F : Oh, I asked for an aisle seat.

M : Did you? Oh, I'm sorry. But don't worry the flight isn't full today.
I will try to rearrange your seat after I check the passenger list.
Would that be alright?

F : Ok.

M : Thank you, ma'am. I'll be back in a moment with a better seat for you.

Chapter 05

Listening

F1 : What would you like to drink, sir?

M1 : I'd like to have a glass of water and a gin and tonic, please.

F1 : No problem, sir. Just a moment, please. Here you are.
What can I get you, sir?

M2 : What kind of fruit juice do you have?

F1 : We serve orange, apple and tomato.

M2 : I'll have apple juice.

F1 : How about you, ma'am?

F2 : Do you have any hot drinks?

F1 : Yes, we do. We have coffee, tea and hot chocolate.

F2 : Can I have a cup of coffee?

F1 : Sure. Do you mind waiting a moment? We're serving cold drinks now.

Chapter **06**

Listening

M : Would you like beef steak or chicken noodles, ma'am?

F : Do you have any fish?

M : No, I'm sorry. We only serve beef and chicken today.

F : Is the chicken spicy?

M : No, it's just mildly spiced with soy sauce. Would you like to try it?

F : Ok. I'll take the chicken.

M : Thank you, ma'am. Would you care for a glass of wine?

F : Yes. I'd like white wine, please.

M : Sure. Here you are. Enjoy your meal.

Chapter **07**

Listening

M : Would you like to purchase any duty free items, ma'am?

F : How much is the Dior perfume?

M : That's 45,000 won, madam.

F : No, I mean in dollars. How much is it in dollars?

M : That's 40 dollars.

F : Can I see the titanium watch?

M : Sure. Here you are. It's 80 dollars.

F : Can you show me the Bally wallet?

M : No, problem. It's 95 dollars.

F : How much are they in total?

M : That will be 215 dollars, ma'am.

F : Can I pay with a credit card?

Chapter 08

Listening

F : Excuse me, sir. Did you call?

M : Ah, yes. I don't know why I can't hear anything with this handset.

F : Oh, I'm sorry about that. Have you checked if your headphones are plugged in properly?

M : Yes. It's just that they're not working.

F : Let me see. Press the volume button here and then the up and down button.

M : Ah, that's it. I got it. Many thanks.

F : You're welcome.

Chapter 09

Listening

M : Good morning, ladies and gentlemen, this is the Captain speaking. We will be landing in New York in approximately 30 minutes.

The local time now in New York is 9:15 and the weather in New York will be clear and the temperature is 23 degrees Celsius or 73 degrees Fahrenheit.

Thank you for flying with Asea Airlines.

I hope you enjoyed flying with us and we look forward to seeing you again.

Cabin crew, please prepare cabin for landing.

Chapter 10

Listening

F : Ladies and gentlemen, welcome to New York. The local time is 9:30 in the morning, Tuesday, October, 17th and the temperature is 15 degrees Celsius or 59 degrees Fahrenheit. Today, we are delayed due to heavy traffic congestion at the airport. We appreciate your patience and kind understanding.

For your safety, please remain seated until the seat belt sign is off and leave all your hand-luggage safely stowed.

Before you leave the aircraft, please make sure that you have all your personal belongings with you and please be careful when opening overhead bins as items may fall out.

We wish you a pleasant stay and we hope to see you again soon. Thank you and good bye.

Appendix 2

2. 기내 필수회화

Boarding

Good morning/afternoon/evening. Welcome aboard.	안녕하십니까? 어서 오십시오.
May I see your boarding pass, please?	탑승권을 보여주시겠습니까?
This way, please.	이쪽으로 오십시오.
Please take the other side.	반대편 복도로 가시면 됩니다.
Your seat is in the back of the cabin.	손님의 좌석은 객실 뒤쪽입니다.
Would you please take your seat when boarding?	탑승하는 동안 좌석에 앉아주시겠습니까?
Would you please step aside to let other passengers through?	다른 승객들이 지나갈 수 있도록 잠시 옆쪽으로 서 주시겠습니까?
I'm afraid you are in the wrong seat.	자리를 잘못 앉으신 것 같습니다.
Your seat is right behind (in front of) this one.	손님 좌석은 바로 뒤(앞)입니다.
May I help you with your bag?	짐 보관을 도와드릴까요?
Could you please put your bag under the seat in front of you?	짐을 앞좌석 밑에 놓아주시겠습니까?
Would you please keep your bag in the overhead bin?	짐을 머리 위 선반에 보관해 주시겠습니까?
We must keep the aisle clear.	통로를 비워두어야 합니다.

Preparation for Take-off

Would you please fasten your seat belt?	좌석벨트를 매 주시겠습니까?
Would you please return your seat back to the upright position?	좌석 등받이를 세워 주시겠습니까?
Could you please stow your tray table?	테이블을 접어 주시겠습니까?
Could you please open your window shades?	창문을 열어 주시겠습니까?
Would you mind turning off your cell phone?	핸드폰을 꺼 주시겠습니까?
We will be taking off soon (shortly).	곧 이륙합니다.
I'll set up the bassinet after take-off.	이륙 후에 아기요람을 설치해 드리겠습니다.

After Take-off

Would you like to use a hot towel?	뜨거운 타월 사용하시겠습니까?
Please be careful. It's hot.	조심하세요. 뜨겁습니다.
May I collect your towel?	타월 가져가도 되겠습니까?
Would you care for something to drink?	음료 하시겠습니까?
What kind of drink would you like?	어떤 음료를 하시겠습니까?
Would you want me to put some ice in it?	얼음을 넣어드릴까요?
May I open your tray table?	테이블을 펴 드릴까요?
Would you like another (one more) drink?	다른 음료 (한 잔 더) 하시겠습니까?
We are serving lunch now.	지금 점심식사 서비스 중입니다.
Are you ready for dinner?	저녁식사 드시겠습니까?
We have beef steak and chicken fried rice. Which one would you prefer?	소고기 스테이크와 닭고기 볶음밥이 있습니다. 어느 것으로 하시겠습니까?
Here is the menu for today's meal.	오늘 식사 메뉴입니다.
I'm sorry. We are all run out of beef just now.	죄송합니다만, 소고기는 다 떨어졌습니다.
Would you like to try chicken, instead?	대신에 닭고기 드셔 보시겠습니까?
Would you care for a glass of wine?	와인 한 잔 하시겠습니까?
Would you like some (a cup of) coffee?	커피 좀 (한 잔) 하시겠습니까?
May I have your cup on the tray?	트레이 위에 커피잔을 놓아주시겠습니까?
Are you done (finished)? May I clear your tray?	식사 다하셨습니까? 치워드려도 될까요?
I'll get it for you right away.	제가 바로 가져다 드리겠습니다.
How are you feeling now?	지금은 좀 어떠십니까?
Another cabin attendant will serve coffee and tea shortly.	다른 승무원이 커피와 차를 서비스 해 드릴 겁니다.

In-flight Sales & Entry Document

Would you like to purchase any duty-free items?	면세품 구입하시겠습니까?
You are allowed to bring one bottle without tax.	한 병은 면세로 갖고 갈 수 있습니다.
They are all sold out. / We have run out of them now.	모두 다 판매되었습니다.
It is 35 dollars in total. / It comes to 35 dollars.	모두 다해서 35달러입니다.
How would you like to pay?	어떻게 계산하시겠습니까?
I'm sorry but we don't accept Indian rupee on board.	죄송합니다만, 인도 루피는 받지 않습니다.
The today's exchange rate is 1,100 won to the dollar.	오늘의 환율은 1달러당 1,100원입니다.
Would you please fill out entry card?	입국신고서를 작성해 주시겠습니까?
You are required to fill out the customs form.	세관신고서를 작성해 주셔야 합니다.
One customs form is enough for each family.	세관신고서는 가족당 한 부만 작성하면 됩니다.

Preparation for Landing & Farewell

Could you please remain seated until the plane comes to a complete stop?	비행기가 완전히 멈출 때까지 좌석에 앉아 주시겠습니까?
We are still moving.	아직 움직이고 있습니다.
We've not reached the terminal yet.	아직 터미널에 도착하지 않았습니다.
Thank you for flying with us.	탑승해 주셔서 감사합니다.
I hope you enjoy your stay here.	이곳에서의 여행이 즐거우시길 바랍니다.
Happy holiday!	좋은 휴가 되세요.
Merry Christmas and happy new year!	기쁜 성탄 되세요. 새해 복많이 받으세요.

Others

May I have your name, please?	성함이 어떻게 되십니까?
I'll show you to the seat.	제가 안내해 드리겠습니다.
I'm afraid there are no seats available on this flight.	죄송하지만, 오늘 좌석 여유가 없습니다.
Let me check for you.	제가 확인해 드리겠습니다.
Thank you for waiting.	기다려 주셔서 감사합니다.
I'm sorry for the inconvenience.	불편을 드려 죄송합니다.
I'll check if we have any left in the other galley.	다른 갤리에 남아있는 것이 있는지 확인해 보겠습니다.
Channel 2 for English.	영어는 채널 2번입니다.
May I turn on your reading light?	독서등을 켜 드릴까요?
Please go back to your seat and fasten seat belt. We are passing through turbulence.	좌석으로 가서서 벨트를 매 주십시오. 기류가 불안정한 곳을 통과하고 있습니다.
I'll be right back.	바로 돌아오겠습니다.
We'll be landing in an hour.	한 시간 후에 착륙합니다.

Appendix 3

Commonly Used Abbreviations in Aviation (항공약어 모음)

1. Abbreviated Airline Terminology

A/C	Aircraft
AFT	At the rear of the cabin
TWD	At the front or forward of the cabin
ATA	Actual time of arrival
ATD	Actual time of landing
ETA	Estimated time of arrival
ETD	Estimated time of departure
STA	Scheduled time of Arrival
STD	Scheduled time of Departure
CIQ	Customs, Immigration and Quarantine

2. Passenger-related Abbreviations

CHD	Child - a passenger above 2 years old.
DAPO	Do all possible - give all assistance to the passenger
INF	Infant - a passenger under 2 years old
PASG (PAX)	Passenger
PSP	Passenger Seat Plan
UC	Unaccompanied children
UM	Unaccompanied minor
YP	Young passenger
VIP	Very Important Passenger
WCHR	Wheelchair passenger

3. Meal-related Abbreviations

BBML	Baby meal - for infants 1 year and below
BLML	Bland meal
CHML	Child meal - for children between 2 to 7 years old
DBML	Diabetic meal
GFML	Gluten Free meal
HNML	Hindu meal
IVGML	Indian vegetarian meal
KSML	Kosher meal
LFML	Restricted fat / cholesterol diet
LSML	Low sodium meal
MOML	Muslim meal
PWML	Post-weaning meal - for infants between 1 to 2 years old
SFML	Seafood meal
VGML	vegetarian meal

4. Abbreviations for documents / reference text / others

ABC	Reference coverage of flight schedules and fares of all scheduled airlines
BSCT	Bassinet
FR	Flight record - a document for flight details
IATA	International Air Transport Association
ICAO	International Civil Aviation Organization
N/A	Not available
N/S	Night stop
TIM	Travel Information Manual
U/S	Unserviceable
VR	Voyage report - a document for reporting on events or incidents

5. Standard Airline Terminology

Apron	An area for parking of aircraft
Block Time	Flight time
Ferry Flight	A non-scheduled flight without passengers
Flight Time	The time of flight from ATD to ATA
Port	Left-side of A/C when looking at the front of the A/C in the cabin
Push-back	An A/C moving backwards on ground using tow-truck
Starboard	Right-side of A/C when looking at the front of the A/C in the cabin
Take-off	When A/C wheels lift off from the runway
Taxiing	Movement of an A/C on the ground under its own power
Touch-down	When A/C wheels come in contact with the runway
Towing	An A/C moving forward on ground using a tow-truck

References

Singapore Airlines Cabin Crew Basic Manual.

Singapore Airlines Air Crew Safety Equipment and Procedure.

이동희·권도희, 『항공실무영어』(새로미, 2010)

김영미·손기표, 『Air Travel and Tourism』(다락원, 2010)

박광희·심재원, 『영어낭독훈련에 답이 있다』(사람in, 2009)

Ellis S., Lansford L. 2010. English for Cabin Crew. Oxford. Oxford University Press.

Gerighty T., Davis S. 2011. English for Cabin Crew. Andover. Heinle Cengage Learning.

사진출처

dreamstime.com

photos.com

wikipedia.org

airfrance.com

emirates.com

thaiairways.com

philippineairlines.com

Singaporeair.com

저자소개   **김수정** Kim Soo Jung

학력
· 인하공업전문대학 항공운항과 졸업
· 한국방송통신대학교 영어영문학과 졸업
· Hospitality Management Diploma at AHLA Hotel Business School
· 성균관대학교 번역 / 테솔 대학원 테솔학과 석사과정

경력
· 싱가포르항공 객실승무원
· 대한항공 객실승무원
· Certified Hospitality Department Trainer at American Hotel & Lodging Educational Institute
· HSBC은행 Quality Assurance Officer
· 현) 아세아항공전문학교 항공운항학부 교수

English for Flight Attendants

2012년   11월 25일   초판 1쇄 인쇄
2012년   11월 30일   초판 1쇄 발행

저 자   김   수   정
발행인   寅製 진   욱   상

발행처   **백산출판사**

저자와의
합의하에
인지첩부
생략

서울시 성북구 정릉3동 653-40
  등록 : 1974. 1. 9. 제 1-72호
  전화 : 914-1621, 917-6240
  FAX : 912-4438
http://www.ibaeksan.kr
editbsp@naver.com

값 17,000원
ISBN 978-89-6183-660-9
(MP3 CD 포함)